Her Reveries and Thoughts

An Anthology of Poems

Nadiya Nizar

To all those who love their own scars as if they are stars,

Who lead a 'one-person' army and are not ready to quit but move on from the pauses to fulfil their dreams –

You're not alone in this. Life will make you flower beds, for sure!! Trust the timing.

CONTENTS

ACKNOWLEDGEMENTS

My Lord, I'm grateful for this life.

1. To my parents and my sister Nourin, you're all I need. Words aren't enough to define the love and support you shower upon me. I would still like to be yours if there is any other possible life available. Know that I love you people more than anything else.

2. To my granddad, I know you would have been so happy now, seeing me achieve my dream. I miss you, and I wish you were here with me. Thank you for your immense love and support. I love you so much. Ummachimma, I love you.

3. To Khadeeja, author of "Subconscious, The Inner Voice." Thank you for guiding me through the right path and for being patient with all my doubts on this. You helped me reach my dream, and I'll always be grateful to you. May you reach greater heights! All wishes.

4. To Sherna and Nafla, I'm so grateful for your friendship. You guys have always supported and loved me. Thank you for being my beta readers. The way you both cheer for me prompts me to do more of everything. Thank you for being with

me in my happiest moments, confused stages, and even in my darkest phases. I love it when we make conference calls to discuss all the dramas in our life and stick together even when nothing goes right. Thank you for proving that distance never separates people. Stay with me forever. And I swear I'll be your best friend till the very end and beyond. I'm so lucky to have you both in my life. Wishing you all goodness.

5. To Henin, I don't know what to say and how to begin. Thank you for coming into my life. You lead me to my dream. May everyone get blessed with a supporter like you. You'll always be my favourite person, no matter what. You get excited for all the simple things I do; it feels like heaven. And I can't wait to meet you in person. Stay happy, stay strong. Sending hugs.

6. To Zalma, thank you for being there for me always. Thank you for letting me know that you are proud of me. You are such an amazing friend. Grateful that I could be my weirdest self around you. I'll always love you.

7. To Archa, it's been only a short while since we've met, but it's like we've known each other for years. Thank you for all the support and love, for being with me in my smiles, tears, and dilemmas, and for

having my back when I thought I was completely lost. How can I express my gratitude towards you for gifting me a brother who is as amazing as you are? Grateful that he too took part in my dream and helped me as if it was his own. Girl, you had stayed up many nights to help me in this, sorting, reading, and re-reading. Forever grateful. You deserve only the best. I love you.

8. To Santwana, thank you for your suggestions and support. You've always encouraged me. I'm so happy to be your friend and sister. You have a special place in my heart, and it'll always remain the same for you.

9. To Reshma, thank you for all the laughter and love. Can't wait to be with you again. Come home soon. Let's make memories.

10. To Sheeja Kunjumma, thank you for supporting my dreams. I remember the day you rummaged through your shelves in search of your old poems that were published in different magazines, and that was an inspiration, indeed. To Mamachi and Mami, I love you a lot. Thank you for making me feel like that old little girl version of myself.

11. To Shiji Mami, you're truly an inspiration. You achieved your dream of publishing a book at this

age, fighting against all odds and overcoming every obstacle. Thank you for accepting me as your own daughter. I love you so much. Write more.

Once again, thank you for gifting me a brother – your son, Shemin. He stood by my side when no one else did. Forever grateful for you, boy. Stay happy, that's all I need.

12. Thank you, Praseetha Aunty, for all the love.

13. Thank you, Soorya Chechi, Gopz, Ponnus, Aishu, and Abin. We are family, and I love you all. Thank you for all the happy moments we had together.

14. To Muhammed M. and Safar N., you both are amazing. Thank you for loving, listening, and supporting me. You both deserve all the love in the world because those hearts of yours are the purest!

15. To Jeevan and Fahadh, I owe you a lot. I love the bond we share! Thank you for making me laugh.

16. To Adal Ikka, Nabeel Ikka, Anzil Kakka, Shehna, Ajimi, Sairu, and Ali, sending hugs and kisses.

17. Little Flock Public School, Kollayil, which laid the foundations for strengthening my dreams and for supporting me all these years.

S N H S S, Chithara, and G H S S, Chithara.

18. The Department of English, N S S College, Nilamel;
the place where I belong. The place that made me
identify myself and my potential.

To all my dearest teachers who guided, supported,
and loved every one of us. Thank you for being
our best friends with whom we can share all our
pains and smiles. Thank you for being with us.
Thank you for making us feel at home when we
were around you. Grateful for all the moments I
had at N S S College. I love you all, a lot.

To all my friends in B A English, we laughed together,
helped one another, and created the most beautiful
years to cherish forever. I remember us talking
nonsense for hours, strolling around the campus,
and being the happiest versions of ourselves. I miss
that. I miss our classroom; I miss all of you.

Super proud to be a part of the legendary
department of N S S College, Nilamel.

19. The PG Department of English, Govt. College
Attingal.

To my teachers, who are always ready to support
their students and never fail to cheer for them;
I'm so proud to be a student of yours. Thank you
for the immense support, love, and care that are
showered upon us.

To my friends in the PG department; I thank every one of you for being with me and supporting me. I love you all.

To my people, the latest ones added to my life, my girl squad of GCA, no words are enough to express my gratitude towards you people. Archa, Abhirami, Ashna, Sradha, Megha, Anjana, Krishnapriya, and Arathy; I love you all. Thank you for keeping me happy. The way we dance, sing, vibe, and rock the stage together makes me happy every time. Thank you for giving loads of memories and happiness to treasure forever. And I want to be with you forever, loving and helping one another and proving to stay together in ups and downs, lights and darks, and throughout the seasons. I love you all.

And Laxx, that 11:11 wish is no longer a 'wish.' It's real, yayyyy!!! Thank you for all the support.

There are more... and I'm thanking all the beautiful souls of GCA who never fail to make me smile. I got y'all.

20. To all the people who left midway; I'm grateful for you all; for not keeping me, for not tolerating me, for not understanding me, for making me feel alone, for gifting me anxiety. I'm grateful that you taught me life lessons, to enjoy my own company,

to make decisions on my own, to go for my dreams and to find time for myself, to do the things that my heart wished for.

It wouldn't be the same if you all stayed. I would have been weak, fragile, and dependent.

21. To all the ones who stayed, who proved – 'not everyone is the same.' Thank you for loving me for who I am and accepting me for what I am. Thank you for the support, love, and those random beautiful words, texts, calls, handwritten letters, and gifts.

~Every person in your life is a lesson. Each of them has a role. Some choose to take the main roles while some go for the guest ones.

Let all of them perform...

Let some of them leave...

And let the others stay!!

01. PAGES OF HER INNER SELF

She's all smiles

and radiated only the same.

A muse with

wide luminescent eyes.

Her inner self was but a mystery,

everyone failed in deciphering

what is kept inside.

And now that mystery

is being unveiled.

She loved

and spread only the same,

but she was wounded;

betrayals made her brittle.

She cared for emotions,

but her inner self was

cowering in a corner,

with no one to console.

Sitting alone,

she listened to music,

which was her medicine,

and cried her heart out

in silence.

Every teardrop penetrated

through her skin and flesh,

but she stitched them with smiles again.

She was happy for others,

but who actually cared for her happiness?

She was waiting to be found out,

but no one came in search of her.

While sobbing without any sound,

she removed the thorns stuck to her.

She bled but smiled,

knowing that she protected

her people from those thorns

by walking herself on them.

She was unique; a sliver of bright daylight

and spread its phosphorescence everywhere.

The smile was her public facade

that made everyone happy but

hid her despairs deep inside herself.

The unveiled mystery is that:

Every page of her inner self turned out

to be love and concluded in a smile.

02. ME

Hug me,

But I'm not voluptuous...

My thoughts are crude

and sometimes urbane.

And you see me

as a monster,

and a Goddess,

at times.

I write,

Pathos... came my lines.

I think,

Perennial... came my thoughts.

The junctures

of my dreams

and reality:

I refilled them with hope,

Again and again.

03. HAPPINESS

Happiness, for her,

Is a hundred little things, not a big deal.

Just some random memories,

songs of her choice,

alms for the needy.

Some smiles, silence at times,

stars, moonlight and the sky,

vastness of the blue sea,

footprints in the moist sand.

The smell of chocolates

and coffee, insurmountable.

Fragments of quotes,

and pages of books,

solace to the wounded.

Thoughts to pen down,

stringed instruments,

again a hundred other things,

They ain't little;

They are emotions, neither big nor small.

She's happy with all that she ever had!

04. HER FAVOURITE SONG

She was a writer,

who seeks charm in lines...

When she listens

to her favourite song,

Hopes that were buried once,

open all graves,

come out,

creep down her neck.

When that favourite line

pops up,

She flies like a butterfly

with broken wings...

tires ,

Falls down and dies.

She pretends to be

alright,

Just to fool herself

and cries in solitude,

asking forgiveness from herself.

Soft-hearted,

then how could she

pray for her hopes,

What if God makes

them true for her?

What if that hurts

anyone out there?

Music healed her,

She was a muse

Of her own world of

mellow melodies...

Melancholic was her heart.

She craved for nights,

to cry, to heal,

and to sleep,

listening to her favourite song,

that made her dream,

Unending dreams of

despair and

beautiful hopes

that never cared for her.

05. LOOKING UP, AT THE SKY

I leaned out of windows
always, just to look at the
sky, like an idiot;
doing nothing, but
staring deeper and deeper
beyond the horizons.
The mayhems were always
made clean when the
starlight reflected inside my eyes.
I smiled every time,
seeing the moon travelling with me
on the darkest of nights.
I counted the stars
with great happiness, called them
by some beautiful names,
that I lost somewhere between
life and death.
The clear sky, bathed in the
daylight, made me enraptured.
I was being brought back

to a small child, innocently

figuring out what the clouds

were shaped like;

fishes, trees, girls, and boys,

And I couldn't help

but watch from a great distance.

The sky drew rainbows for me,

as if it had known that rainbows were

my favourite hopes.

If there existed moon princesses,

then I would like to be the next.

Running away from pain

and getting intoxicated in the sky,

I found myself a happy place,

where I forgot about a world

existing around, and encircling me.

I stared at the sky,

like I was the only being there,

drowning among the clouds now,

and living among them, the next moment.

06. SELENOPHILE

Yesteryears of loneliness
found me as a selenophile,
who gazes at the midnight sky
with two gleaming starry eyes.

Lunar lover and her maids,
clouds of dark and early stars,
And I was falling for,
all over, once again.

The moon was perfect,
silver skin, flawless in
each imperfection, and
you made me find myself
that I was flawless in my flaws.

Haunted me, those moonless nights
as I'm searching cloud by cloud,
Moonlit sky was paradise
as I'm waiting for the nights.

Nadiya Nizar

Oh Moon!! You made me find myself

that I was flawless in my flaws.

Let me scream that you are mine,

"My sun, My moon and all my stars"!!

 Her Reveries and Thoughts

07. HER REVERIES

She was a girl who strolled

down the valleys of her reveries,

where there were flowers and

butterflies that filled the landscapes.

She was a girl, living in her

own little world,

realities apart, she dwelt peacefully.

Such a space granted her freedom

and made all her desires come true.

She watched the babymoon,

exultant of all the shimmering stars around.

And she believed in celestial nymphs

and shooting stars,

'cause she was living in her reveries,

far from realities.

In the daylight, she ran after

the scurrying butterflies,

competing for the wildflowers.

She wore them in her curls

and danced as though,

she was a fairy princess,

waiting for her prince to come

and to live 'happily ever after'

in the resplendent letters

of an opulent fairytale.

Sometimes she made herself

a witch - not so ruthless -

but just to cure her wounded heart;

preparing magic potions

and chanting spells and being invisible

to visit those places,

forbidden only for her;

And meeting the one,

she wasn't able to but always wished for.

And was granted invisibility,

because she was still living in her reveries.

When emptiness spread itself

deep inside her, she tried to

fill the vacuum with hopes.

She walked through the promenades,

all alone ('cause she was the only

human in her reveries), humming

          Her Reveries and Thoughts

her favourite song.

Fingers crossed, she awaited

for unicorns and rainbows every day.

And it happened one day;

But with a hollow heart,

she watched the brightest rainbow

falling in love with the pretty unicorn.

The next morning, she felt dewdrops

on her long eyelashes,

cold and spherical,

gleaming by the rays.

She lay down on the green grass

which bore yellow flowers,

and started writing a poem.

She made everything she loved, eternal,

through her lines.

But she was mortal,

no one wrote anything about her.

Was it too much to wish

to be written about?

But she knew, no one ever will.

She spread her wings

and flew among the clouds, carefully,

without getting distracted from her reveries.

But somehow collided with

realities, her wings vanished,

And she was floating in the air,

struggling hard; she woke up.

It pierced through her heart,

But then she was amazed,

because, reveries apart,

there she had a beautiful poem,

on the paper.

08. BOOKISH

Whenever I felt numb,

I searched for books on the shelf.

Whenever I felt happy,

Then too, I searched for them.

It was my emergency exit from a world of worries.

I lived in phantasmagoria,

where everything was comforting,

but there too, had chaos which made

my eyes well up with tears.

But I loved crying through pages,

Because there I forgot all my despairs

And cried for people who hardly breathed in the real world.

Sometimes my sanguine thoughts failed to make it right

when the noxious things happened unexpectedly.

And it made me realise that life is no different.

It never worked sanguine every time,

but took turns and hills when I expected them the least.

I never felt like an interloper among pages,

as I was someone witnessing everything along with

the characters.

I had loved many of them,

Knowing that they are inanimate.

But it was way better than loving someone in real.

No complaints, no heartbreaks,

And no images, of course.

It's me who gave them faces, shapes, and attires.

And I was happy that I could change them whenever

I felt I can't handle it anymore.

No more adjusting, not tolerating,

But changing from books to books

And pages to pages

in search of my better match.

Books made me dream in colours all around.

The letters made me figure out my own existence

among those fictional beings.

But they were better than any other human who lived

out here.

Every person in those pages taught me life lessons;

they made my imaginations lively.

And to the living,

Who create these non-living humans,

"I'll be forever grateful,

that you people opened me a world

where I was not alone and depressed."

09. THE SUICIDE

Suicidal thoughts? Yes,
but not in that tattered
old, typical way.
Just different, it was.

When everyone chose
ropes to strangle
themselves down; I
opted for 'pen' where
I was strangled by words,
choked to death
by creating poems.

Some grabbed blades
to cut through veins,
while I grabbed papers
to cut through my thoughts.

And when they opted
for poison bottles,

 Her Reveries and Thoughts

I searched for
bottles of Ink.

Some of them tried
ending themselves up,
while I was weaving
life in my lines.

My 'escape exits'
were my suicides,
I was letting
myself free,
And I never hurt myself;
'cause it's my body
that carried my soul.
And it's a trap, killing
yourself.

Choices will be there,
but you are the one
to choose.
You only live once.

Verily,

Better decisions are

made through

varying options,

and it's up to you!

10. THE FUNERAL SONG

The path was crowded,

like it was a festive season;

But it was a funeral,

tears suffused the air.

She was sleeping

inside the coffin.

Every passerby wondered,

asking who were all those,

crying on her demise?

They belonged to different ages,

castes, lifestyles, social status,

and gender.

Everyone had their own words:

"She had helped us,"

"She made me live my life,"

"She used to fill me with hope,"

"She stood by me when I was down,"

"Her words healed my mind,"

"She was the happiest among us,"

and it was endless like an ocean,

an ocean of teardrops.

The people who asked

got their answers,

and they felt that

the girl in the coffin reminded

them of something:

"Do good; only your good deeds speak.

It's something great if you receive

some genuine tears as your last gift."

And those random minds were moved;

They also walked away with tears,

Each drop was for that unfamiliar

girl who had lived the greatest

life, indeed.

11. VOIDS

For those who are dead,

it was nothing after all,

Because no one knows what happens

after carcasses are mixed with soil.

But for those who are still alive,

It's hard,

They have to live then,

with memories of the dead.

They are actually the grieving.

How can someone fill

a void created by another?

Realising the one who danced

with you late nights

is no more;

their name

and some blurred memories

are all that is left,

hurts?

And the dead are not going through

depressions, memories, and thoughts

as they're already dead.

Their emotions died along with them,

their thoughts and their bodies too.

But voids are created from then,

differing in shapes, sizes,

and places.

The void created by a best friend,

the void left by someone's lover,

the void of a mother

or a father

or some 'annoying' sibling

or any of someone's beloved.

It can't be refilled

with someone else.

The void in classrooms,

the void in bedrooms,

the void in a silent kitchen or in doorways,

the void we feel anywhere;

It can't be replenished.

   Her Reveries and Thoughts

For everything, living

or not, there are voids.

And I think,

we only own some voids,

without realising it when we're alive,

and we won't realise it,

even after our death,

Because voids are impersonal,

it can only be felt by others.

Someday, I too will create a void,

without really knowing

who will be living in my memories

afterwards.

A crowd is fine,

and so are laughter and noises.

But emptiness is scary,

and the ultimate silence left by someone

is quite scarier.

Nadiya Nizar

12. THE SCARS

There are scars all over,

neither cried nor complained,

I accepted myself.

Every scar has a story to tell,

So that this unidentified romantic

was never been so lonely.

Freckles and pimples,

chronicled the days and ways,

And so, this thoughtful being

lived in her own world.

Beauty lies in hearts,

That's why this hopeful lover waited;

Waited for someone with scars all over

and a heart to accept her, the way

she does it herself.

13. YOU

There in my words, thoughts,

dreams, I found you...

Even the little bit of beats

craved to rest on your lap.

Feelings for you, not so tentative,

but unnerving deeply...

Heart pounding... Fumble sighs,

Just congenial

to this hallowed intoxication.

And I realise,

Every bit of me has you...

14. A RANDOM LOVE POEM

It is the fake scenarios that made her laugh

Like an idiot.

All the moments in her dreams were happier

With him.

Love is invisible at times,

Not palpable, yet breathing through dreams.

Without knowing, they knitted the same scenarios

From different places.

Smiling for nothing,

Music echoing in everything,

She lived among dreams,

Where everything was better

With him.

And she made poems

That was her love language,

Which made everything clear,

But not for everyone.

How beautiful it is,

To dream of someone

And smile at that thought.

 Her Reveries and Thoughts

Perhaps she also wished for someone

To dream of her,

Along with the lyrics of some

Random love songs.

15. IF I DATE YOU...

If I date you,

I just want to be with you, at times,

Without any other needs,

but just to stare at you.

I know, I'm expensive,

but not for you,

I just want to capture the

feeling of being loved.

If I date you,

I'll never say

'no' to your happiness.

I'll be fighting for your

passions, as you do.

If I date you,

Know that, you've got a

comfort zone, where you

could be weird, happy, relieved,

and even silent and emotionless.

If I date you,

You've got a listener;

Your past stories

are not gonna

haunt you anymore.

If I date you,

I'll never claim you,

'Only mine';

I know, you are not

only mine.

You have family,

friends and self-time

to take care of.

If I date you,

You don't have to

search for rings and gifts.

You love stargazing?

That's romantic, and
I won't demand for
anything else.

If I date you,
You've to put up with
me, always expressing,
'How much you
mean to me.'

If I date you,
I'll be sending you
my playlist, and
you too have to.

If I date you,
Know that, you are
not going to be chained,
You can do whatever you want.
You won't be asked to
be within my sight.
You can have fun,

You can sit alone,

You can hang out with friends,

You can do it all,

'cause I'll be loving you for what you are,

And that's more than enough!

16. THE CUPID AND HIS ARROWS

When I first saw you,

I think no Cupid was around.

I just looked at you,

And that's all.

Then again, when I saw you,

I think the Cupid forgot to aim the arrow,

Because I was at ease.

But when I got to know more,

the thought of your smile created something unusual in me,

and stirred up my emotions.

My nights became sleepless,

and daydreams running through my head all the time.

I don't know why, but I wanted to see you, hear you.

And when I saw you for the next time,

(It might count as the hundredth meeting).

For the first time ever, I guess the arrow got struck right into my heart

and scratched your name in rough letters.

It was hurting a little,

but I would say:

"Oh, it was my favourite pain though!"

I was never at ease from then.

I've heard of Cupid's arrow getting struck for once

and making people fall in love for the rest.

But mine was different,

Cupid was playing tricks, for sure.

I was getting struck by arrows again and again

but over the same person.

Everything about you was an arrow aimed at me.

My heart was becoming a quiver

that stored arrows of different varieties,

the arrow that made me fall,

the arrow that struck me when you smiled,

the arrow that made me think of you,

the arrow that was aimed at me when you looked at
me

straight in my eyes,

the arrow that pierced me whenever you talked,

the arrow that was for nothing,

but to remind something was happening to me,

every now and then.

But I'm grateful for the Cupid,

for all the arrows;

that it made me know more of you,

helped me fall in love with you again and again

and to treasure every little thing about you.

Oh, Cupid, trick me again,

I love the pain of arrows piercing my heart.

17. THE DREAM

It's the moon who prompted me

to love you again,

to dream all the possible ways,

but like a fairytale.

All night,

I dreamt.

The beautiful moments

I never experienced;

The damp seashore of my dreams

where I gazed at your eyes

and drowned myself in.

Without any words,

we sat still,

lost in love.

The starlit sky,

the moonlit waves,

shimmering sand,

seashells,

and the cold breeze that blew

the hairs on your forehead.

I felt everything

like I was living the moment.

But when the moon hid behind

the clouds,

my dreams shattered,

he was nowhere,

And I was left alone on the shore

of realities.

18. EMERALD WINGS

In the stillness of

a mundane day,

the bud turned

into a flower,

exultant of her

beautiful petals.

Then for another

minute, her eyes

got stuck on,

a pair of emerald wings.

She detected the ebbs

inside herself.

Was she falling

for a butterfly

she just saw before?

She was waiting

for him to visit her.

The palpitations increased,

as she saw those wings

flying towards.

Her petals quivered

at the touch.

Along with the nectar,

he purloined her dreams also.

Intoxicated, she was, for

the first time ever.

But those wings were

searching for other flowers;

prettier and sweeter.

She sobbed in the emptiness of nights.

Witnessed her dream,

shattering into a thousand

little pieces; impossible to fix.

With a heavy heart,

she realised,

her moments were being counted.

She was just a flower; short-lived.

The next morning,

With some remnants of

hopes inside,

her first petal flew up, then

Slowly, fell downwards.

                    Her Reveries and Thoughts

She was withering

down, all her petals,

then as a whole,

she touched the soil;

Her pale eyes focused

on those emerald wings

on another flower.

With tears,

she held tight,

the image of the emerald wings,

once again; just before

closing her eyes,

for the last time.

19. BUTTERFLIES

You gave me butterflies,

but I acted like you never did.

Should I express my love,

for that it is not mine?

Do I endure pain,

knowing that you won't come my way?

I tried to forget,

got ended up remembering...

I was afraid to change...

I thought I can't.

But,

No more a girl of fantasies,

You never valued me;

Why should I waste my time on you?

I know, it hurts,

but thought that

it could give me infinite peace.

Peace, I always longed for...

Seasons wheeled around,
Wounds began healing.

No one ever knew,
that you gave me butterflies once.

It was a nightmare,
And every such nightmare
ended when dawn broke,
And now, My dawn too...
Nightmares never happened then.

I'm happy that
I moved on.
"Fly away from the tree,
which never valued you,
Even if it is filled
with flowers and fruits."

I got my bosom broken,
and I can't blame you...
You never knew, how

deep it was...

Are you aware of my existence?

I know you aren't.

And I didn't want you to.

'Cause I'm not that girl anymore.

My stomach is not

a butterfly garden.

But know that,

No one ever can give

me butterflies anymore.

I've got a

venomous visceral after

your butterflies left there.

20. THE FALL

The spring of your heart

is beautiful...

But I'm the autumn,

fallen and drowned beneath

the soil of your dreams.

I wished to bloom inside you,

creep through your emotions,

sprout as a smile on your lips...

I failed,

Broken,

You own a spring

and that's not mine...

I'm the fall,

that ended up under your feet.

21. JUST A HUMAN!!

The embers of love

Spread like the stars,

Millions and millions...

But where it failed?

Did I forget to embrace your mind?

I don't know,

And you never let me know...

I'm just flesh and bones,

And incapable of reading minds...

No superpowers, just a human,

Living in fantasies,

Like any other.

I loved and now realised,

I'm just a human,

Don't expect more from me,

I've got no wings,

But only flesh and bones,

Know that,

Injuries do happen to me too.

22. HOW MY HEART BREAKS!!

I thought I forgot

But still I remember.

They were illusions

flickering before my eyes.

I wished

not to be found;

'I never deserve'

Somehow, I convinced that

lover inside my soul.

Existence never screamed

my name,

Nor did your presence.

It is quite natural

to be unnoticed;

I suppressed my emotions.

Only my pen moved,

it never reached you,

And I didn't want it to.

You are that closed book

with strange letters,

I tried reading

But you were not ready

to rest in my heart,

Slipped out of my embrace,

You left,

Letting me freeze.

I don't intend to read you again.

I'm afraid to open you once more.

You are not a perfect fit,

for my weeping bosom,

which I call a bookshelf.

Again, I convinced myself

'I don't deserve you,'

And that's not the truth

I know.

23. PAIN

Meet me
where we met for
the last time and
walked away with
drooping heads,
tear-filled eyes and
a broken heart.
But now I wish,
You are here...
Still, I've feelings for you,
immersed in the pain of love.

24. GETTING OVER YOU

The moon loved me,

he gave me the stars...

But my heart craved for you,

You got me nothing,

But pain,

tears,

and some fragile dreams...

How can I reset my mind,

my thoughts?

How can I love the moon?

My heart still craves for you,

Love me at once,

Or help me reset my mind!!

25. ONE LAST LOVE POEM

It's me,

writing one last

love poem for you.

I've preserved bundles

of love, just for you,

But, now I'm bleeding love,

feeling all the pain,

with watery eyes.

Whenever I wrote 'love'

the shimmer at the tip

of my pen drew you.

You have room in my heart,

tarnished, it may be;

you never visited there,

that's why!!

I wished not to

write of you anymore.

But it's me

writing again,

the last love poem.

Sometimes it suffocated

me to death.

Images of you prompted

me to write more.

Wretched,

Broken,

I fetched you in papers.

Now, I'm giving up,

writing this last love poem.

It's me,

writing one last

love poem for you.

Still conflicting with my

emotions to make

this the last poem on you.

But I know,

It can't be.

The wound, you are!!

The medicine, you are!!

My pen, paper, and emotions, you are!!

'One last love poem,'

But my heart aches

and says

"It can't be."

26. GOING THROUGH THE CHANGES

Whenever the river flooded

over the banks and

jumped over the soil lumps,

I thought of all the old days,

when we both were innocent children

running by the banks

barefooted,

bare-hearted

without any thoughts

covering our eyesight.

Immense happiness flooded

the banks of our minds,

every monsoon,

just like the river.

Years passed,

the riverbed cracked up

leaving a thin stream

amidst the cracks and stones.

We met again,

          Her Reveries and Thoughts

not as two innocent children

but as two fellows with

secret chambers inside their hearts.

And then our eyes met,

not with smiles on lips

but with some unsaid words

remaining on the lips

and reflecting in the eyes.

Those minds were cracked up

just like the river,

leaving a thin stream

amidst the emotions and actions.

We didn't say a word

nor faked a smile.

And we kept those unsaid words, unsaid;

(It's beautiful keeping such words inside.)

They both walked away

without turning their heads

for that last eye contact.

But they left two souls behind;

The souls of two innocent children,

They were hugging each other

and crying

without wanting to be separated again

and unable to say their last goodbye.

27. WHY DON'T YOU LOVE?

Why don't you love?

They asked.

My inner self stuttered

Unable to find the proper words

To make it an answer.

I was afraid to love.

I know, if I fall

I'll fall harder.

My heart can't unlove, it just loves.

The fear of losing someone

Had always haunted me.

And whenever I thought of

loving someone, the same

fear appeared inside my chest,

creating erosions and eruptions.

I can't let go,

Delicate is my heart!!!

It loves.

I'm weak when it's love,

I'm fragile when it's my beloved.

Nadiya Nizar

And I believe, overthinkers

Like me are easy preys.

They're easy to cheat on.

Because they fall for hearts.

Then how do you write love poems?

They asked.

My heart was love itself.

My mind contained a whole lot of it.

Imaginations are limitless

So, I imagined,

Fetched it in papers.

I never wanted to hurt anyone.

My ideals were simple,

Finding someone to grow old with...

To hold those hands even after they form wrinkles,

And loving the same, till the very end.

28. RAIN THOUGHTS

(i) You love rain? They asked.

It was my way of thinking about you;

All the betrayals and broken relations

made me love the rain,

to reassure, after every droplet

there came another one,

after the blue-black clouds

there came rainbows.

(ii) The first drop sanctified

the dry earth,

and the shower embraced

with all its love,

leaving me intoxicated

by the fragrance of soil.

(iii) Rain itself made me forget

all my despairs.

Rain is my counterpart,

who was waiting for her turn,

with dreams and desires inside

to shower all of them.

(iv) And for the very next moment,

when she got to shower,

all the hidden tears

were uncovered to the soil,

getting rid of a burden;

with happiness, embraced again

and made ripples of hope.

(v) Leaving droplets on grass blades,

Thunderbolts of her heart - silenced;

lightning sparks in her eyes - faded;

Getting deliverance from all the pain,

with indelible marks on the soul,

The rain - she eventually died

among the clouds.

29. CROWD

At times, it felt like

the crowd was the safe place to fit in;

Veiling up emotions and

being one among the hundreds.

But at some point,

the crowd was like a monster,

which made me cower in corners;

trembling, stuttering and

being left alone among the hundreds.

30. THE GARDEN OF PAIN

I planted a garden with flowers that bloomed

irrespective of the seasons.

Varied in colours, fragrances and aestivation.

But this garden of mine hid behind its formosity

a lot of pain, unnoticed by many.

Each flower represented each of the pain

that my weak heart was unwilling to explain.

The glorious sunflower faced the sun till the dusk;

And that pain of mine faced me throughout the days
and nights.

Some of the flowers bloomed in the darkest hours of
the nights,

and those were my pain that arose only when the rest
of the

world was sleeping, peacefully.

The cacti that fenced my garden walls were assumed
to be strong,

but it was a pain that pricked me with its sharp
thorns,

tearing my heart every now and then.

The green sods seemed to be moist for everyone,

but it was just another pain where all my plants bloomed

upon molten lava that heated up my inner emotions.

There were some other plants that failed to bloom,

just like my favourite pains which failed to prove their reasons.

There were butterflies flying around pollinating my flowers;

They were the factors that pollinated my pains,

connecting them between the wounds.

The garden seemed beautiful to everyone,

but as the gardener, I was the only one who knew

the pain behind every flower.

It was the garden, invisible.

I was keen to cultivate it inside my mind.

Everyone assumed me to be a beautiful garden

filled with happiness and fragrance;

But deep inside, I was watering the plants

which were wounds and pain.

Every person is a garden from the outside,

but pain from the inside,

healing alone in the corners of solitude.

31. THE TOOTHLESS SMILES

A medley of memories,

Rushing past my inner self;

Fragile, it may be

But purloined all my sorrows.

Walking through the hardest phase,

I knitted together my childhood days;

Pondering upon the smiles,

Toothless and

Painless.

Gobsmacked by small and

Little things,

I had days of joy,

But reality pricks me now,

For I'm an adult

Engaged in a forever war with

Dreams and actions.

Nothing amazes, this adult,

Nor the small fishes, flowers,

Crayons and watercolour palettes.

Pain was considered trivial then,

Now it attacks me;

All claws and talons.

Warm cardigans were knitted with

Grandma's love,

But yesterday the green sods

Sprouted a small flower

Above her chest.

Seasons wheeled,

Memories too.

And all I want back is my smile,

Which was not my usual mask

To hide up emotions.

There once was a little heart in me

Which rejoiced and jumped for joy;

Now being caged by ribs

As it is ferocious to tame down.

Motherly kisses, fatherly cuddles,

And mischiefs; turning out to be

Laptop, workload

And wounds,

Bleeding out every time.

My thoughts ran back again,

Halted where I met my first love.

Memories began to flow.

First love was joy,

Which was lost somewhere

But never strangled me.

Now 'love' hurts, it entwined me with

Thorns

And gifted me scars all over.

Happiness recently,

Seemed tentative

Which gave way to palpable grief

I swear.

My sighs came fumbling,

Stuttering and at times,

Out of breath.

Indeed, childhood was hallowed;

As adulthood feels like 'Halloween',

Scaring me unexpectedly.

What more can I ask,

Other than my childhood?

Would it be so insane to wish

To go back to my happy places?

I had wondered about my adulthood,

Always dreamed and wished;

But now I want those moments back,

Catching butterflies in the garden

Rather than killing some butterflies

Flying around my viscera, inside my stomach.

The dots and mazes I resolved were easier

Than the actual life mazes, which lead me nowhere.

Now I realise, it's too late to say,

But let me scream out:

"Those toothless smiles were beautiful;

Imperfect but perfect in all ways"!

32. WISHES

I heard a slight murmur

of wishes being granted,

But my voice stumbled

upon my thoughts and decisions,

for all the losses were mine

And I wanted every such

loss to be made a gain.

Everyone went back

with happy faces, holding

those wishes that came true.

I was standing still

for all the wishes inside

my head were too heavy

to be carried forever,

but I got no place to rely.

I too had wishes,

innumerable, so none of them got granted,

And it's good that nothing was

granted for me,

as I never wanted only a part

of them being fulfilled,

If it's happening,

then every wish of mine

has to be granted,

or else I don't want anything

as they are absolute equals

for me; having the same values.

33. TO HEART, FROM MIND

To the heart,

which lives inside the same body;

I'm writing to you,

just to console you

and to stitch your wounds.

Listen, you are still stuck

on those people who left you,

for no reasons.

You loved, but they betrayed.

Don't you know,

you had survived long ago,

you had thrived silently when

you needed someone the most.

Whenever I warned you to be

careful about getting attached to people,

you never did listen.

I know you can't

as you are - heart -

the centre of all emotions.

You loved everyone

even after they betrayed.

But why can't you think

that they don't miss you.

Dear heart, realise it,

they didn't value you,

that's why they left midway.

I've always wondered about

the shelter you are provided with.

You are kept inside a cage of bones,

well protected but fenced.

Now I know, you are fragile

so you've to be sheltered,

And you connect easily

with other people; so you are fenced.

Look at me, I only own a name -Mind-

Even I don't know where I belong or

what I'm supposed to look like.

Being judgemental is my way,

but you never did, you only loved.

Your frequent breakdowns

affect this human too.

Nadiya Nizar

She is struggling to keep both of us

bonded together.

I feel sorry for our human.

You've a tight schedule

to work continuously,

then how do you get this much time to think?

Just focus on your works,

you are getting too emotional these days.

We both have seen many times,

our human crying hard alone.

And then my decisions would be selected,

but over and over, every time

you put your emotions on top for her,

to pick up,

letting her cry harder.

I'm not making you desperate,

but strong.

How many times you've been screwed up?

Numerous!!

But make this, the last

and move on.

You are too pure, so is our human.

You love unconditionally,

and that makes you distraught.

At times, I hear you,

beating faster.

Those palpitations make me fearful,

expecting a sudden detonation,

and we are all dead;

You, me, and our human.

I'm elucidating it clear again:

Can't you see this human

crying and trying to compromise

and returning back getting her

wounds torn wide by everyone?

I've told her many times,

but she listens to emotions and

the flesh inside the cage of bones.

Try making her understand

her self-worth,

and you too,

realise your value.

Remember, when we both tried together and

made her survive her darker days;

But now, it's the darkest, I know,

sombre, sunless, and starless

her days and nights are.

Don't be timorous,

we've a long way to go.

I just want to make her happy

and I know, you too want to,

But you are stuttering

on your words and decisions.

Chaos attains patterns at times,

Now, patterns are to be made.

And my friend,

I value you,

Our human too values you.

Love can be given

but cannot be bought back!

I think, you got it.

Words are meagre with me,

and this farewell is not

an actual farewell,

as we both will be together with our human.

Much love,

'The mind',

which lives somewhere

inside this same body.

34. WEAPON

Words - The weapon that
cuts throats.
Without heeding to
blood spills, it moves on
to the next row of throats.

Every human, living
Every carcass, in soil
Every spirit that wanders
were victims of this weapon.

The boneless tongue,
sometimes ruthless,
kills hopes and dreams
throwing words towards.

In between the conflict
of 'heal' and 'hurt'
some tongues lost their
ways - from innocence to murderers.

Words heal

So as they hurt.

To hurt is instant,

Just a throw,

the weapon could

cut through the skin

And even stab one's heart out!

To heal, takes time.

Weapons with blunt edges,

Roses, daffodils and

an entire spring...

Don't throw,

But gently press it to the

chest of the other.

Help him breathe the

fragrance of words; now

not a weapon it is!

Words are puppets

that sway for the tongue.

Mastering the use of

those puppets could

go for an entire life;

But still you may not

master the use.

Be careful with every word.

Be careful that your puppet

won't stretch out of

its strings.

Be careful,

They are sharp

And they can kill.

35. UNWRITTEN RULES

It was said to smile all the time,

Even when I was sad.

I wanted to cry but they forbade as it was

For the weak.

I was fed up with all the unwritten rules.

It was then I realised that humans fail

To see what's inside hearts.

They always get attracted towards the externals

And frowned with contempt

When someone never matched their visions.

The crowd told me to laugh anyways,

But scolded when it was louder.

So, I kept quiet, without uttering a single word.

Then they wanted me to speak

Because it's not good to get muted before others.

"Check on your attires" they pointed out,

I put on colourful clothes.

"It's too much; pompous" they stared.

I changed it to some dull ones

Then they smirked and said "you've got little colour
sense".

They added their opinions in

Whatever things I have done.

But when I started to tell mine,

They stopped me as I was still a 'child'

Immature and senseless.

I took it to heart

And when I did something wrong

They criticised me as I was an adult;

Fully grown up and capable of doing everything

Without making any mistakes.

When they saw me after some time

They sympathised, "eat more, you're too lean."

So, I ate more, then they complained,

"Oh! You're obese, eat less."

I lost my appetite.

"You're dark!"

"You're too pale!"

But it was me who didn't see

Any differences in skin shades

But more concerned with the love they had for others.

They never allowed me to be alone

As they were 'afraid' that I'm against 'people'.

So, I made a lot of friends,

Then they blamed me for having so many of them

For that it is 'dangerous' for me!

Nothing went right with society

For they had rules to impose.

When someone questioned the rules

They argued to accept it without asking.

Unwritten yet ruling with strength.

I just wanted to sink to the bottom of the earth

Or just fly away to where there are no such people!

But learning to live with them was a challenge

That made some of us 'better humans'

And love everyone without heeding to these rules!

36. A DEEP BREATH IN

Inhale,

Exhale.

"Your pain is no bigger than mine."

"Oh, but your wounds didn't need stitches."

Yes, they're right,

I know.

I sighed.

"Our room had no doors,

but walls all around; at least you had

a crack in the wall to look outside."

That's true too.

I prepared to move my lips, at last:

"I'm sorry for all your loss and pain,

I'm sorry that your wounds were egregious,

morose and the silence that followed you.

And I'm thankful,

I've never been through

what you've been.

But the truth of it all is:

I only know my pain,

Because I have endured,

maybe less than yours,

But it's pain too.

You can only measure

what you've experienced.

And you haven't experienced

what I have.

Every 'pain' is 'pain'; better or worse,

take a deep breath in

and accept it.

You know not what someone is going through

because you only live your life.

Again,

Take a deep breath in,

think twice,

then judge,

if you still want to."

37. SILENCE

"A seeker of silences am I,"
penned Gibran,
I too was a seeker of
unsaid words.

Those words buried
deep down in the soul
were heavy;
I can't express nor share,
the burden I carried,
inside my weak mind.

Silence, it never seemed
empty and never left
a single void.
Silence was a chant,
A charm itself.

It had answers,
questions, and emotions

Left unsaid,
But conveyed more than
what an uttered word
could ever do.

"A seeker of silences am I."
I found solutions in silence,
questions in frowns when
there wasn't even a single word.

Soiled feelings,
I silenced them,
As my mind was aware,
words will kill.
I lived years with silence,
Won over every sound,
Now it's death, silence hereafter,
Unsaid words, I buried in my soul.

You couldn't read my silence;
The paradise or hellfire,
whatever it may be, getting

ready to be silenced,

with the arrival of the seeker.

You couldn't read my silence,

Now it's death, silence hereafter.

Maybe you are not supposed to know

what my silence meant,

and how it ended up.

38. TO LET THE WORLD KNOW MORE

Have you ever felt like losing?

Have you ever felt like being alone in the crowd?

Have you ever wanted to cry out of nothing?

Everyone demanded it to be 'depression';

Simplified and babbled as if it was an honour.

But not for the real ones who endured.

Because it was a bird of prey

Clasping its talons into the heart.

Depression was not as it was glorified on screens,

It hid itself in the host, carving the flesh.

The smiles that coloured the pale faces were a facade.

And everyone believed it.

Failing to see the unseen,

And to hear the unheard.

The world made 'anxiety and panic attacks' simple
and nothing.

They sang it out loud as if it was a melody.

Have you ever given up on your food as anxiety
sucked up your hunger?

Have you ever felt that tension in your stomach

That rises up to your throat?

The simple things, feeling not so simple,

Having sleepless nights without any dreams,

Scary, right?

Chaos, mayhems and palpable feeling of nothingness

Creeping all over, jabbering chants of a subconscious mind.

This is to the society that judges every face without considerations:

"Everyone is not the same as they seem to be,

Every mind is complicated,

At times fighting invisible wars.

Physical injuries can be sensed,

But not the ones in the mind.

It's not simple.

And just stop making it to be.

Heal everyone,

It costs nothing but a few words."

And for everyone who fought back to live again:

"I see you,

You're strong,

You're loved

And you deserve to be."

39. THE MISSING PIECE

She touched her nose with a shivering finger.

Blood was oozing down towards her torn lips.

She wiped it off, tired and sobbing.

It was not the first time,

But at least, this time the pain of the wounds felt less.

Maybe because the previous time,

She got fractures in hands, a broken jaw bone

(Ah! Yes, the same jawline he praised during the first
days of marriage),

Torn lips, a bluish under-eye,

And scratches made by her favourite vase, that she
bought from the fair, yester night.

Which drew puzzle mazes all over her tanned brown
skin.

She loved him,

And he never did.

The so-called marriage system stamped her mouth

And tied her hands.

He was that ideal man, outside their walls,

But a wild animal in treating her.

She never thought of some random news-story happening in her life,

And one day she would also become a victim of abuse.

How could any girl reject such a charming gentleman?

So she confirmed it with a happy "yes," checking from all perspectives.

But who knows, liars and murderers never let any aspects doubtful.

She thought of leaving him,

But her love for him never allowed.

And she believed in him, in his fake promises and all the lies,

Even if she had known the truth.

She wished to be the love that would change him in all ways.

But it never happened.

The urge to leave him strengthened.

But the ignominy of being husbandless made her stay back.

She feared society judging her,

Way more than she feared him.

And she never wanted to be blamed for all the faults
being hers.

How could her parents accept her?

They married her off,

And now how could they take all her responsibilities?

And there, she stopped her decision to leave him.

She began to drown among the waves

Of horrors, of her past days of marriage.

It was a Saturday night,

When the beast appeared for the first time.

The malevolence glinting in his eyes

Made her a coward, who couldn't help but cry.

She felt too weak in his strong arms.

Everything began to fade away,

All that she could see was blood.

Stitches made the flesh together,

But not their hearts.

It was his first 'sorry' that deceived her.

But later on, knowing it all,

She accepted the sorries.

She wanted to move on,

But failed every time.

Trust was uprooted somewhere

And liquor took its supremacy.

Her breath was erratic with fear,

Hollers never reached the walls.

She saw her friends enjoying on the shores

With their men,

And what else could she do other than

Finding lies and shutting the windows.

She tried to talk away everything so far,

But his propensity for violence drew her back.

Somewhere between, she realised

Love can't be left,

Some people fall harder and they fail to go back.

She regretted all the moments in her past,

When she blamed people for not leaving.

Now she was stuck.

Finding a way to live without his face

Became a long-lost puzzle.

It was a breezy morning,

Forcing her eyes open, filled her with pain.

Walking past the mirror, she saw a woman

Lean and not so human.

She wept over her reflection.

She couldn't imagine herself before the marriage.

Her eyes were swollen,

Throat was hurting,

Some new scars,

Unevenly cut hair,

Red and blue patches over her shoulders,

A cut on the lip,

Now it tastes like fresh blood.

Numbness and pain all over.

She wiped off the tears,

Walked silently across their bedroom

Got some of the colourful clothes,

Thrust them into a bag.

The water was cold, it hurt her

As she washed away the drowsiness.

It was only then she thought, tying hair into a low bun

Can also cause pain.

She walked out of the room, silently,

Without waking him.

She was afraid to turn back and look at him sleeping,

What if it changes her mind?

It was her last day with him,

She knew a piece was missing,

It was love,

But lost long before.

And she was unaware of the next path,

But she was determined not to return to the old one.

40. HOPE

Hope is optimism, I would say.
Now it dwells in my soul,
where a broken heart once was
waiting for its cadence back.

Aphorisms never seemed precious,
as my bosom was heavy,
swooning and imploring
for deliverance
from all the despairs, worries, and sorrows.

My eyes then beheld hope,
It imbued my soul
with a mellifluous vista
of hope itself.

Transient smiles were
made redeemable.
Obscurity turned to congruity,

I began believing in

the beauty of the future once more.

Hope,

You are my forever.

Your assent made me live again.

You replenished my soul

and gave my heart its cadence back.

41. THE SHOULDER

The bus was crowded,

a medley of people sighing and panting

off the dreary summer day.

Somehow, still through the rush,

I found a window seat.

As music was my relief,

I plugged in my headphones

escaping from reality.

The scorching rays pecked my cheeks,

whereas the lyrics poked my heart.

Minutes after minutes,

songs after songs,

I was dreaming with eyes wide open.

Somewhere between the languid sights and blurry
dreams,

I felt someone sitting next to me.

A lady with a heavy bag placed close to her chest,

her curls fluttering in the wind,

and she was too tired

that her eyes were falling shut.

I could feel her forcing them open

but she failed every time.

Concentration and priority switched from the lyrics

to that lady who was still struggling to stay awake for
a while.

And now she lost all her senses,

the sweetness of sleep embraced her weak eyes.

She was swaying,

and for the next moment,

I felt her head on my shoulders.

She was sleeping peacefully,

and I adjusted myself to make her comfortable.

It hurt a little,

but my heart never wanted to wake her up.

Seeing her sleeping on my shoulders

made me smile.

My daydreams came to an end,

But I liked the way I watched her and made her sleep
comfortably.

She opened her eyes at times.

But closed them with ease.

I tried not to disturb her even in the turns and jerks.

After some more minutes of sleep,

she shook off the sluggishness, stood up,

and went out without turning back.

I don't know her,

And I didn't want anything from her,

even if it is a feeble smile.

My heart was full,

a palpable happiness was surrounding me.

But I knew one thing,

these little big things made me smile,

they made me feel worthy,

and they prompted me to love more of myself.

The lyrics became audible then,

but I was still smiling for that unknown lady

who left her sleep midway.

Nadiya Nizar

42. TO THE BOY UNKNOWN

The morning was too loud, the city rushing through the eyes of people,

Where no one waited for others.

Life was busy as it seemed to be.

My eager pupils focused on a weak, wrinkled lady

Eating her food from a plastic bag

Occasionally looking at the passers-by,

Begging with a stretched, veiny hand

Shivering and murmuring in a strange language.

I was curious to know more about her;

Her home, her near ones,

And the reason behind her being on the sidewalks,

All lost and alone.

But I always ran late,

Just looking at her and throwing a smile

On her way.

But my mind wandered around her,

Patiently waiting for some day.

It was some other day,

As usual, I was running late.

The city rush was making a trance in my head.

The chatters of the children in uniform were loud.

And there were lovers holding hands and smiling
gently.

The traffic signal winked, and a sphere of crowd

Crossing the road,

Competing with one another.

I reminded myself of the college bell,

So I was in a hurry.

But before passing the road,

I turned my head to check on the wrinkled face.

And my eyes caught something else;

There was this boy sitting on the bare, dusty
pavement

Facing the lady.

He was listening to her,

Unconscious of the world around;

Smiling, keen, and all ears.

Nadiya Nizar

He seemed to ignore all the city rush,

The traffic, the people walking around him.

And some were adjusting themselves to walk

Through the pavement as he was blocking it.

I turned my head, twice, thrice;

The sight was making me warm,

Producing something sweet

Flowing from my heart.

Everyone was busy,

Including me,

But there was this boy taking his time

To hear others.

And it refilled my trust in humanity.

People are different,

Still, there are people who have good hearts.

Boy,

I don't know you, nor your name, nor where you live,

but I know your heart.

And I think it's the best link

one human can have with some other - The link of
hearts.

People like you are rare,

and I wish all the goodness on this earth

and beyond to shower upon you;

You deserve it.

This is to the boy unknown for making me trust in
humanity once again.

43. PEACE

Feel the unseen world

with eyes closed;

Music on,

listening to heartbeats,

Finding all the

broken pieces,

Knitting them

together;

Reveries and peace at last.

44. THE ARBOUR

I belonged to an arbour
deep inside my own soul.
But someday, I left there
and came out of that
beautiful bower,
for some people, believing
that they could build me
a better place to live in.
But later, I got avoided
by them, knocked on
their doors and at last,
I turned into a vagrant
lingering between the
old memories of my
arbour and its aroma.
With an inflamed heart,
I walked back, finding
the path with a quest
for life inside.
After loitering

hither and thither,

I found the arbour;

started living there,

and never left.

The arbour was inside

my own soul, where

I was myself.

From then, I never walked out

for others, with expectations.

I was happy within the arbour,

sinking deeper

into my own soul.

45. WHEN I FOUND MYSELF

When the thoughts of my heart

turned into words...

When the starlit sky made my soul

leap and bounce around...

Then the world seemed colourful,

Every wound healed...

As I walked down the lanes,

more hands caressed...

After all, I was a happy being,

with some melancholy as her music.

46. SELF LOVE

The chaos of the daydreams
choked me,
The horrors of the nightmares
haunted me,
Until I loved myself,
Then the world greeted me.

 Her Reveries and Thoughts

47. A POET'S HEART IN A GLANCE

As I was drowning into my dreams,

my pen moved,

to fetch my bleeding words,

to the limitless papers...

It seemed alright for everyone,

But not the same for poets

As they were aliens,

trapped in human bodies...

For a poet, just as frenzied

as I am,

I longed to live forever

in the castle of holy letters.

When the disarrays suffocated me,

I again controlled my fumble sighs

to look upon eternity,

Still, it chooses me - As I am a poet -

"Gobsmacked" I yelled at

my own words

Because it was always me

who admired myself.

Tornadoes, hurricanes, earthquakes

and what not,

Every inch of earthly pleasures

and of course celestial matters,

beyond the imaginations, muses,

witches and magical potions,

I concluded everything at the

tip of my pen - As I am the poet

Fervour always, to choose

my escape world,

deeper into pages, where

I was the fairy, hero,

Alice, Juliet, and Cleopatra.

It was not tentative,

to be a poet - It was life itself -

I found myself intoxicated

by the words encircling me;

I'm not dead yet, and so won't be,

My words are eternal, so as I am.

The crevices of my heart

flow ink,

Happy that I am a poet with

some hallowed hurricane of words.

48. THE POETIC INJUSTICE

Are you real?

Do you even exist?

We've never seen you in poems.

No one writes about you.

But you write everyone as if they are poetry.

Indeed, they are!

But how can you tell they are real only

Because I write about them.

Sometimes I give them qualities that my

Mind desires for.

I give hearts for the heartless,

Voice for the muted,

And songs for the dead.

I create humans who are actually not one.

I dedicate love poems to the ruthless

Unromantics.

I paint hearts with white,

Even if they are dark,

Unlike their skin.

It's me who make them poetry.

They may not write about me;

But at least I'm real as I create

beautiful beings

through poems.

And everyone says that they are poetry

And I'm unreal as I'm not written about.

49. SURVIVOR

Macabre,

Curvaceous,

No more a living being.

Endured,

and happy now,

that I chose myself.

Living my kind of life,

Nothing more,

Nothing less,

I adore myself.

50. THE GRATITUDE NOTE

I know it's not enough, but words are all I have.

So here I am, leaving a piece of gratitude

for all the ones who have my heart.

Throughout the dark, irksome nights,

I cried without having an ear to listen.

I searched for a shoulder to rely on,

And never found one.

The dearth of love and companionship made me

Question myself.

I doubted my own heart and soul.

I loved to talk a lot,

And laugh more,

But had no one to do it with.

I did everything to keep them

As I was afraid to lose people.

But every one of them left,

Making me feel worthless and

Denied of love.

It was when I started to sit alone

And tried to understand myself.

Realising my mind and the dreams

I had buried once, gave me new roads to explore.

I counted the people who were still there,

Less in number.

But they were enough.

This is a piece of gratitude to those people

Who gave shoulders when my head was drooping down

With sorrow.

My heart was moving away from attachments

As if it was scared of them.

But there came some souls who made my heart

Capable of having attachments again.

How can I express my love towards such people?

Words are all I have!

Grateful for holding my hands and never letting me fall.

Grateful for wiping away my tears and planting them with smiles.

Grateful for standing up for me when no one else did.

Grateful for giving me time, space, shoulders, and ears.

Grateful for shattering my fears and shackles.

             Her Reveries and Thoughts

Grateful for laughing with me,

And crying with me.

Grateful for making me realise myself.

Grateful for expressing how much I mean.

Grateful for letting me know that I'm loved and
valued.

Grateful for trusting me, understanding me, and
reading me when

I was silent and wordless.

Grateful for helping me run for my dreams.

Grateful for the loud and silent cheers and applause.

Grateful for all the little big things.

This tiny heart is so full.

And there is no room in it

For holding grudges and angers.

It is love, more and more of it.

And I'm spreading it,

Along with these words.

EPILOGUE

To my readers,

This may not be the most beautiful poetry collection you've ever read, and I may not be one of the most refined writers you've ever come across. But what you've read now was once a reverie; a reverie of an ordinary girl.

(Yes, I had reveries of publishing my first book, and now I'm elated that it is getting fulfilled!)

This book has my heart, and I'm giving it to you all, to keep. Thank you for being the most important part of my journey, my dream.

Go for your dreams; no matter how big or small they are, just chase them.

With love,

Nadiya N S.

www.ingramcontent.com/pod-product-compliance
Lightning Source LLC
Chambersburg PA
CBHW032020140726
47988CB00017BA/701